FARM ANIMALS

by Gallimard Jeunesse
and Sylvaine Pérols
Illustrated by Sylvaine Pérols

A FIRST DISCOVERY BOOK

SCHOLASTIC INC.
New York   Toronto   London   Auckland   Sydney

As the sun comes up,
a rooster crows loudly to wake up
the people in the town...

...and the other
animals on
the farm.

Roosters, hens, ducks, and geese
look for worms, grain, and other food.

These farm animals are called fowl.

Hens are female chickens. Roosters are male chickens.

When a rooster and hen mate...

Rooster

Hen

There are many different kinds of chickens.

. . . chicks will grow inside
the eggs the hen lays.

The hen will care for the chicks
until they are strong enough
to go out on their own.

The hen shows her chicks
how to peck the ground
with their beaks to find grain.

Ducks are clumsy fliers.

But in the water,
  ducks are very
      graceful.
    They dive . . .

A male duck

A female duck

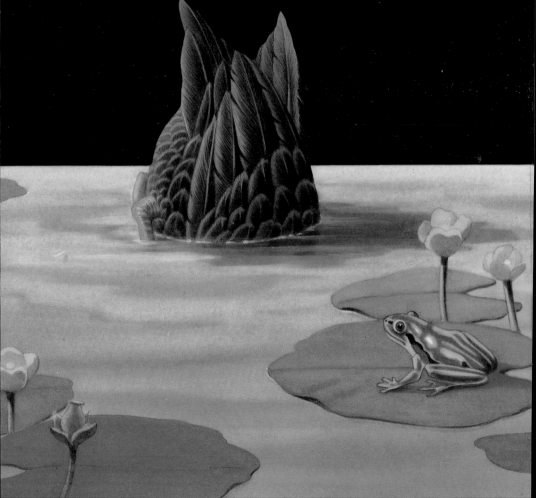

When ducklings are born, they are covered with soft down.
In about one month their feathers grow in.

...to eat the plants that grow
on the bottom of the pond.
Their web feet act like paddles
to move them through the water.

Geese travel
in large groups
called flocks.

When a goose feels
threatened, it stretches
its wings and neck to look
larger and scare its enemy.
It does not have teeth
but its beak can pinch
very hard.

During mating season, the male goose dances to attract the female.

The mother teaches her babies,
called goslings, to swim.

She shows them how and what to eat.

Turkeys have loose
red skin on their
necks called
wattles.

Guinea fowl make loud noises.
Some people keep them to scare
away strangers.

A male turkey
fluffs up
his feathers
to impress
a female.

Rabbits hop from place to place. They have very strong legs.

One rabbit stands guard
and listens for danger
while the others eat.

These two males are dancing around
to attract the female for mating.

What is inside this cage?

Newborn rabbits cannot see. Their eyes open
and they grow fur in about 10 days.

It is a
mother
rabbit and
her three
babies.

Many different kinds of farm animals
can share the same pasture.

Look at all the different kinds of cattle.

Bulls are male cattle.

Oxen can pull
heavy loads.

Cattle eat grass and hay.
In the winter they may eat grain.

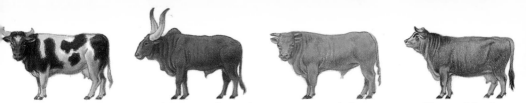

Some cattle are raised for work. Others are raised for meat, milk, and hides.

Cows are female cattle.
They produce milk
to feed their calves.

The milk
that
we drink
is collected
from cows on dairy farms.
It is cleaned by machines.

People raise sheep for wool, milk, and meat.

Each spring sheep's wool
is shaved off. This does
not hurt them at all.
The wool is spun
to make yarn
for knitting
and weaving.

Sometimes farmers use working dogs
to keep sheep from wandering away
from the flock.

A male sheep has horns and is called a ram. The female is called a ewe. Young sheep are called lambs.

Sheep eat
mostly grass.

There are many kinds and colors of pigs.

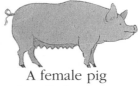

A female pig
is called a sow.

A male pig
is called a boar.

Pigs use their noses,
or snouts, to find
food to eat.
They love to eat!

A curly tail is the sign
of a healthy pig.

Some people think pigs are dirty animals, but they are really very clean. They only roll in the mud to keep their skin cool on hot days.

Isn't a farm full of wonderful animals?

A sow can feed as many as 14 piglets at a time.

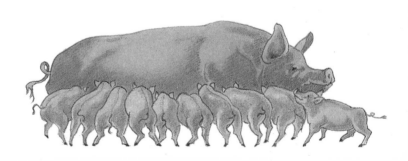

Library of Congress Cataloging-in-Publication Data available.

Originally published in France in 1992 under the title *La Ferme* by Editions Gallimard Jeunesse.

ISBN 0-590-11618-5

10 9 8 7 6 5 4 3 2 1   8 9/9 0/0 01 02

Printed in Italy by Editoriale Libraria
First Scholastic printing, August 1998